I BELIEVE IN YOU!

STORY BY
SABRINA MOYLE

PICTURES BY
EUNICE MOYLE

WORKMAN PUBLISHING * NEW YORK

WHEN SOMETHING'S NEW,

WHEN YOU'RE READY,

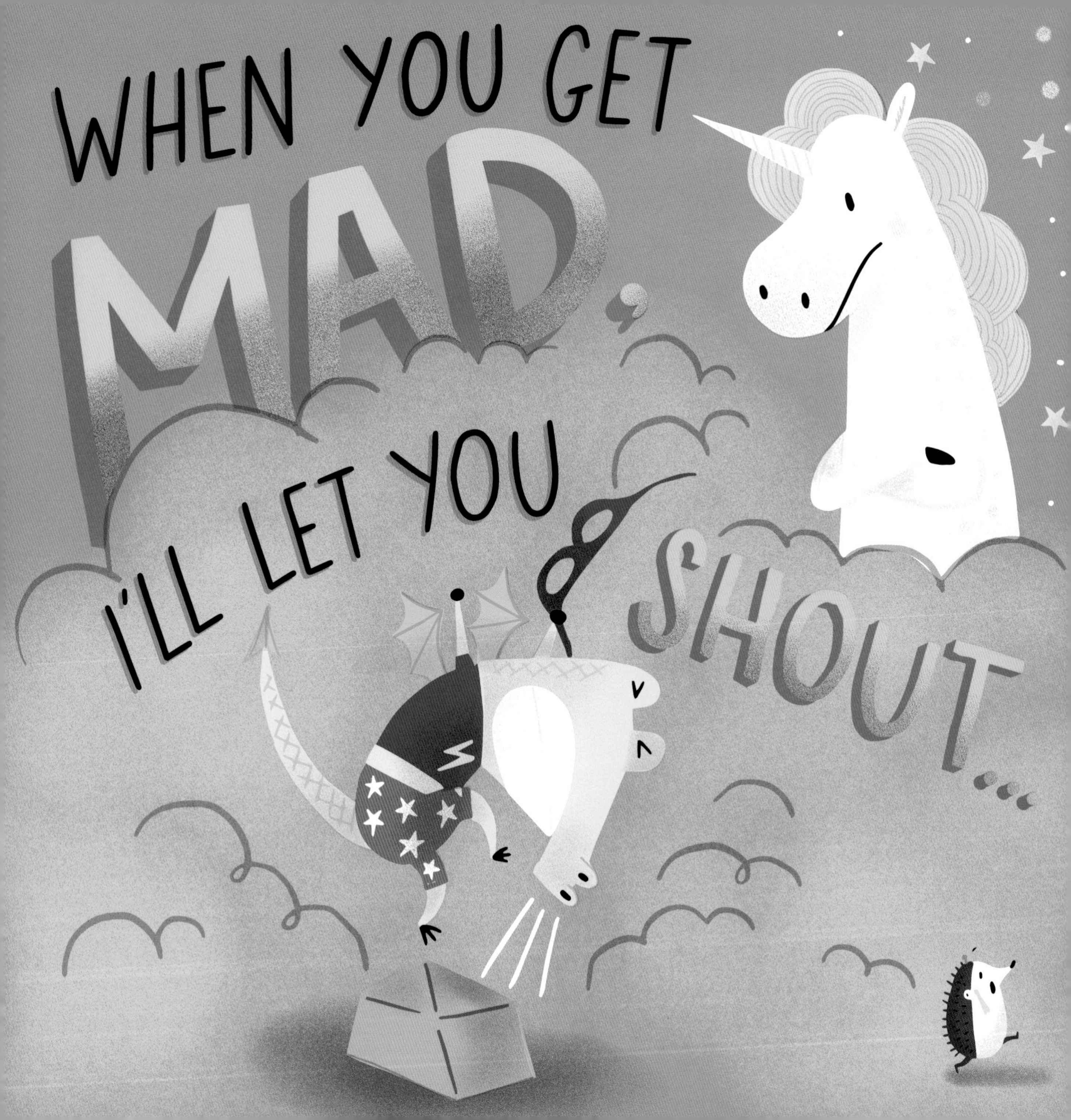
WHEN YOU GET
MAD,
I'LL LET YOU
SHOUT...

IF YOU FEEL SAD,

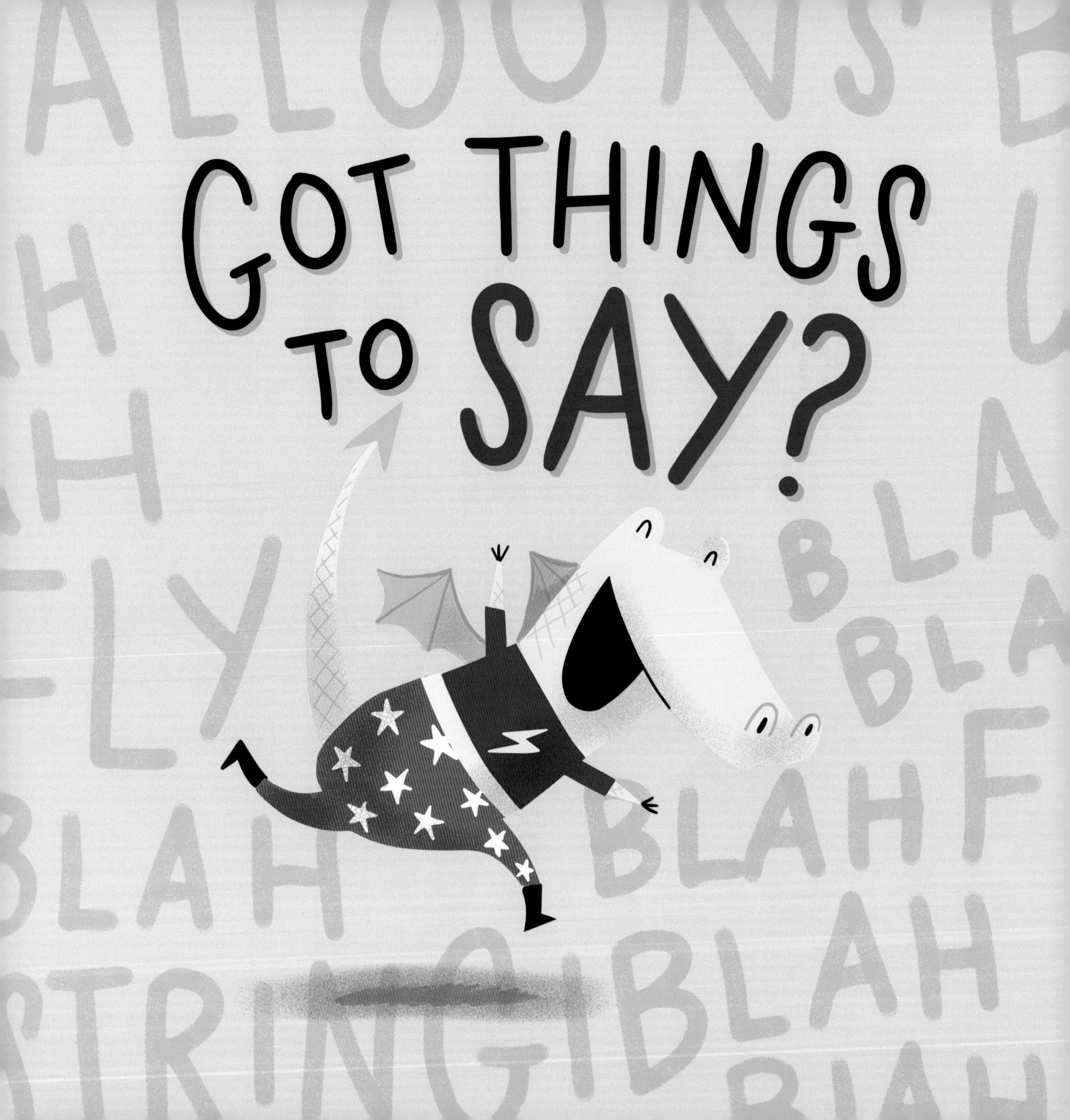
GOT THINGS TO SAY?
BLAH
BLAH
BLAH
BLAH
BLAH

WELL, I'M ALL EARS!

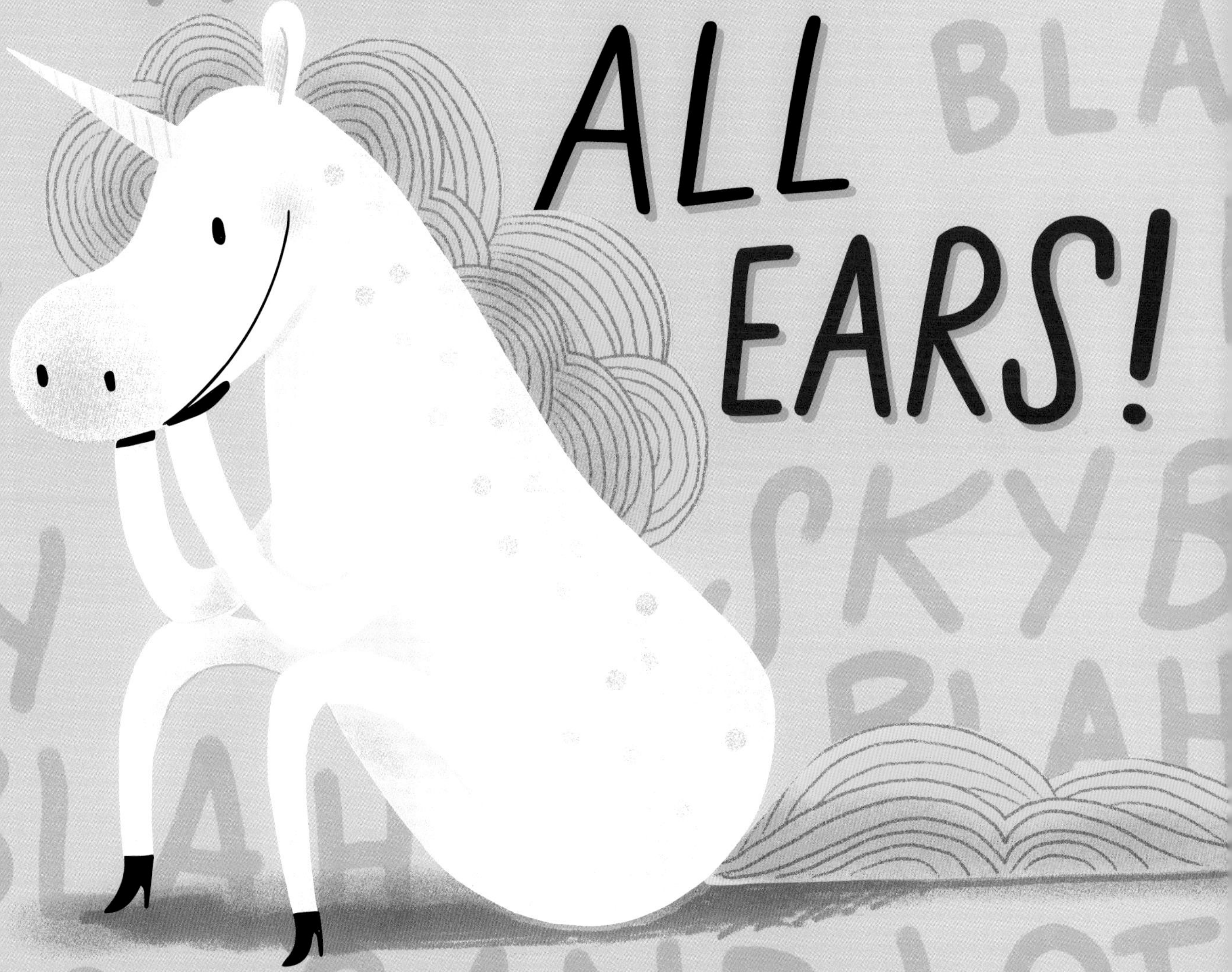

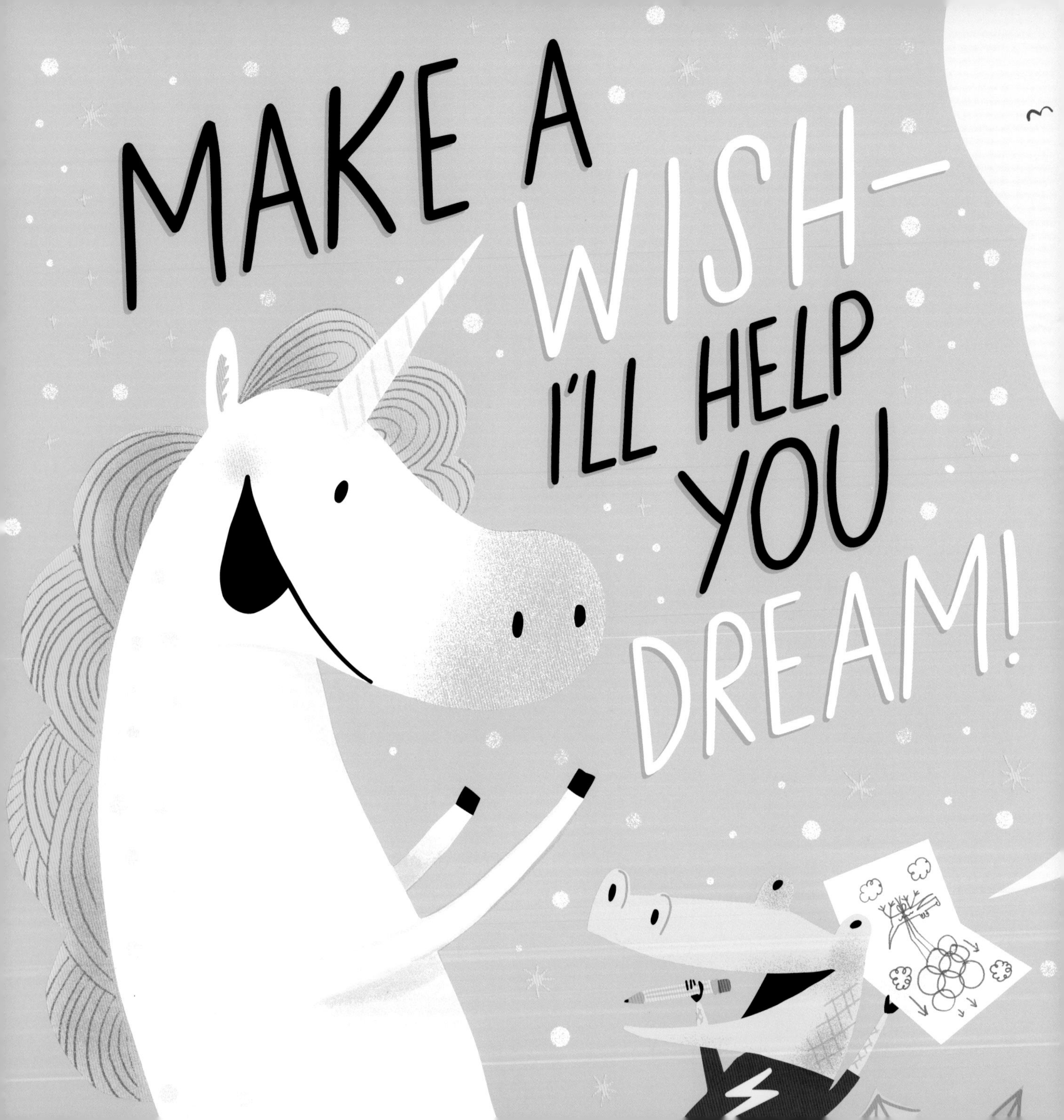
MAKE A WISH—
I'LL HELP YOU DREAM!

TAKE A
GO ON AND

CHANCE, TRY!

AND IF YOU

FALL,

THAT'S **OK**,

TOO!

MATTER WHAT
DO...

FOR TRACI—
THANK YOU
FOR BELIEVING
IN US.

Workman books are available at special
discounts when purchased in bulk for premiums
and sales promotions as well as for fund-raising
or educational use. Special editions or book
excerpts can also be created to specification.
For details, contact the Special Sales Director
at the address below or send an email to
specialmarkets@workman.com.

Workman Publishing Co., Inc.
225 Varick Street
New York, NY 10014-4381
workman.com

WORKMAN is a registered trademark
of Workman Publishing Co., Inc.

Printed in China
First printing August 2020

10 9 8 7 6 5 4 3 2